Mama's Cookbook
A Memoir and Recipe Book

By Frances Flores-Sentino

Copyright © 2022 by Belifuna, Inc.
All rights reserved. This book or any portion thereof
may not be reproduced or used in any manner whatsoever
without the express written permission of the publisher
except for the use of brief quotations in a book review.

First Printing, 2023
ISBN 979-8-9875576-0-0

Acknowledgments

First, I would like to thank my parents, Stanley and Louisa Flores, for instilling faith and a love of reading in me. They were my biggest supporters and taught me never to give up on my dreams. I'd also like to thank my former mentor, Sister Mary Lynn Fields, for empowering me during a difficult time. May they all rest in peace.

Thank you to my daughters, Dían and Díónísía, as well as my siblings, for their love and encouragement throughout this process. Thank you to my dear friend, Francis Reyes, for his love and friendship since First Form in high school. And a special thanks to Selma J., who started the writing class at our senior center, for encouraging us to tell our stories and publish our work. She has published two books and is working on her third.

Finally, I thank the team that made this book possible. Thank you, Carolyn Birden, for teaching me how to proofread my work and helping me proofread the first draft of this book. Thank you, Dan'l, from the Women's Press Collective, for taking the time to type Carolyn's edits. Lastly, I'd like to thank my daughter Dían for being my editor and publisher.

Table of Contents

Why I Write	1
Introduction	3
Part I: Growing Up in the Flores Family	7
Home Cooking	9
Blue Crab Season	17
Hurricane Hattie	21
My Parents Taught Me to Pray	27
Part II: The Cookbook	31
Meal Planning	33
Sample Weekly Meal Plan	37
Mom's Recipes	41
Basic Sorrel Drink	42
Split Pea Soup	43
Meatballs in Black Sauce (Reano Negro)	44
Green Banana and Cornmeal Porridge	46
Coconut Crust	47
Banana Bread	49
Green Banana Pancake	50
Pumpkin Bread	51
Green Banana & Pink Salmon Cake	52
Pesto	53
Black Fruit Cake	54
My Mom's Stewed Green Papaya	56
Cassava Pudding	57

Table of Contents (cont'd)

Cabbage Salad	58
Festive Rice	59
Spinach Rice	60
My Version of Scones or Irish Soda Bread	61
Fruit as a Side Dish or Dessert	62
My Bean Dishes	62
Part III: My Nutrition Workshop Notes	**63**
About the Author	**71**

Why I Write

I need to write because I have something to say and much to offer. When I am happy, I write. Writing down my many blessings fills me with joy when I feel sad. I can also change my mood and outlook on a situation by writing.

There is so much around us that we can look at positively or negatively. I want to write about it all! I like to write down information I want to remember or share with others.

We are all connected and on this earth for a purpose. Writing gives us a record of events, tools to use, and evidence to leave behind for our loved ones to know more about us.

- Frances Flores-Sentino

Introduction

My wake-up call was when my doctor told me that I was prediabetic. My recent bloodwork showed that my A1C level was 6.2. According to the Centers for Disease Control and Prevention (CDC), the A1C test measures your average blood sugar levels over the past three months[1]. Your doctor uses your A1C to determine if you are prediabetic or have diabetes. A normal A1C level is below 5.7.

I was shocked that I was prediabetic because I have always been particular about what I eat and have never been overweight. Walking is a part of my daily routine, and I climb four flights of stairs to get to my apartment. I also practice yoga and attend aerobic classes regularly. After doing some research, I learned that my diet was the problem.

I first heard about the A1C test and prediabetes at the senior center, where I attended aerobics and yoga classes. After my diagnosis, I asked a few ladies how they enrolled in the course. Some of the other women had taken a course for prediabetics at a local community center. My friend, Selma, told me that the current class began the year before and was almost over. She gave me the phone number to call

---

[1] https://www.cdc.gov/diabetes/managing/managing-blood-sugar/a1c.html

and register for the class that would start in September 2017.

When I called to register for the prediabetic class, I was 116 pounds. At the time, whenever I weighed myself, I was always one or two pounds less than before. The woman I spoke to told me they were only taking people who were overweight, but I refused to take no for an answer. I needed help to stop losing weight! This class was also important to me because I wanted to share what I learned with my friends and family in Belize who were struggling with diabetes. The woman finally gave in and added me to the class.

After reading *A Brooklyn Guide to Healthy Eating* by Brooklyn Borough President Eric L. Adams in 2018, I was reminded that although researching diabetes was good, I still had to do my part. Mr. Adams wrote that reversing hypertension and many other health conditions may be possible if you begin to make healthier eating choices. He recommended starting the practice of putting the right foods into your body. Mr. Adams also shared many resources in the pamphlet, including the book *How Not to Die* by Michael Greger, MD.

It seemed like diabetes prevention and management were the hot topics on TV and in the newspapers then! I am grateful that I had all those resources available to me. It was encouraging to learn how to take control of my health.

The first day of my class for people with prediabetes was Thursday, September 14th, 2017. God blessed us with an excellent coach and instructor. He was also prediabetic and had taken the course before. The class and my independent research inspired me to reflect on how my mom handled food challenges and modify some of my favorite recipes. I decided to write this book to share those memories and recipes.

Although I found these recipes helpful in my health journey, I am not a doctor or nutritionist. Please consult with your doctor before making any changes to your diet!

Frances Flores-Sentino

Part I
Growing Up in the Flores Family

Frances Flores-Sentino

Home Cooking

As a child, my parents made sure that they and all seven of us children had three meals a day. The house always had different kinds of fruits based on the season. My parent's home in Seine Bight Village had a private beach in the front and a lagoon in the back. The lagoon was full of mangroves that grew at the water's edge. You could fish or catch crabs from the front or back of the land. None of us had the patience to stay long enough to have enough fish for a meal, so we always bought fish from the local fishermen.

We had coconuts on the beach in front of our home. We all liked to gather dry coconuts for cooking and baking or young coconuts to drink fresh coconut water. I mastered the art of making tablata (candy made from grated coconut, spices, and sugar) at an early age. You can add canned cow's milk to make it creamy.

When I went to high school, I was happy that I had the skills to make a few goodies to sell and earn my own pocket money. One of my classmates in high school wanted to learn how to bake a cake. I offered to teach her if, in exchange, she would teach me how to sew a pants skirt.

My family also had two large sea grape trees and one almond tree on our beach. At the back and sides of our house were mangos, cashews, sweet potatoes, okra, sugar cane, plums, and craboo, a fruit also known as nanche. We also had a Caribbean blueberry tree and cassava in our yard for cooking or baking puddings.

When we were away from home because Dad was teaching or the principal of a school in another part of the country, we always had a garden in the yard of the house provided. The parents of the children who were fishermen or farmers sometimes shared their extra fish and produce with us. There was usually a chicken coup with roosters and hens in the yard. When we needed eggs, we had them. No one in our small villages had to buy chicken because we raised them ourselves.

Dad would buy our staples such as flour, rice, sugar, beans, milk, salt, and salted pigtail when he went to the main town to cash his cheque. He usually brought back the fruits that we did not have at home. When we were in Cocal, we bought fresh fish from nearby fishermen. My Mom made our clothes, fresh coconut oil, baked goods, and even our birthday cakes. The fruit preserves, homemade wines, and fruit drinks she made for special occasions were always a hit at our house! I looked forward to inviting my friends over, and we always had enough food to share.

When I was eight years old, I enjoyed learning to cook by watching my mom or older sisters cook.

They often made Garifuna dishes like Tapo, made with fresh fish and sliced green banana cooked in a gravy of roux or coconut milk. We added whatever vegetables we had in the house or our garden (usually okra, cabbage, or green papaya) to the gravy.

The other easy dish to cook was green banana dumplings, which we would have with rice or rice and beans with stewed chicken. After grating the green bananas, we would add pepper, grated onions, and salt to taste while the coconut milk was boiling. I liked a lot of pepper in mine!

We added the mix to the boiling gravy one spoonful at a time. We also made tamales, which are like Puerto Rican pasteles. My mom would cook the corn and grate it in a corn mill. Next, she seasoned the corn and added coconut milk with a pinch of salt. She would mix the ingredients and then place a pot spoon full of masa on a green banana leaf. Then she would flatten the masa and place stewed chicken on top of it. Next, she would fold it in half and tie a piece of banana leaf around it to keep the tamales together. Finally, she would steam them for an hour.

The best part of cooking was baking desserts Saturday evenings. There was always some kind of cake, powder bun, or pudding (either potato, pumpkin, or corn) available. Sometimes we would make a savory version of one of the puddings and have it with meat as a meal. All six of us girls and our brother would help make dessert. One of us would grate the coconut while someone else cut the wood for cooking, mixed the batter, or washed the pots and pans. Mom would say, "We will all help, and we will all relax and enjoy what we made on Sunday."

Mom made the best powder buns! Even now that she is no longer with us, not one of us has been able to make them the way she did. I am good at making tarts, tablata, cakes, buns, cross buns, or sweet rolls. One of my sisters is good at making puddings and a hand full of Garifuna dishes. We all learned how to make the dishes we liked best and made them our own.

There was always something to do around the house, and we had time to read or sew in the afternoon. Most days, I would volunteer to do the baking, cooking, or gardening. Each child washed their clothes in a big wooden bowl used only to do laundry. We were also responsible for cleaning the yard by raking, sweeping, or pulling up grass, depending on what was needed most. At least two of us would go to gather firewood. My siblings and I often traveled in pairs or groups of three because we were not allowed to go anywhere alone.

We gathered as a family at home on Wednesday nights to pray the rosary and practice songs for mass. Dad almost always led a prayer service on Sundays; we, the rest of the family, were the choir. I learned public speaking because my father encouraged us to prepare a poem, song, or story for the family Sunday afternoons. How I wish all young people could spend quality time with their siblings and parents as I did!

My childhood home in Seine Bight Village, Belize.

This tree is on the beach in front of my family's home.

My sisters (L-R) Christine, Louise, and I.

My sisters and I, with our brother Matthew's son:
(Back row, L-R) Florence, Louise, and Sr. Joan

My siblings and I in New Orleans celebrating Sister Joan's 60th Jubilee on June 8, 2019 (L-R) Louise, Christine, Matthew, Sr. Joan, me, and Florence.

Blue Crab Season

There have always been many Blue Crabs in my hometown. My mom usually prepared them for eating, but I was more interested in catching them! I caught the crabs using a kisskiss, a homemade tool like tongs made from the wood of a palm plant. It was fun to wait by their hole and play cat and mouse with them. I would wait patiently for a Blue Crab to move away from their burrow and then grab them with the kisskiss and put them in an empty rice sack. On good days we would find a few crabs hiding behind fallen trees.

When we did not catch enough crabs to feed the entire household, we put what we caught in a small drum or large bucket. We would make a small opening on top so the crabs could get air. After a day or two, there were always enough crabs for the whole family.

Mom or my oldest sister, Julia, would cook the crabs we caught in a big pot. When the crabs were ready, Mom would remove their shells, season the meat, put it in a crust, and bake it to make crab pie. That was always a treat! During sea crab season, we had those to enjoy as well.

My siblings and I looked forward to gathering firewood for cooking and baking. In the summer, we would find abandoned beehives that still had honey in them. The older children showed us how to find honey instead of beeswax. At other times we would also find delicious wild plums

My parents were two of the kindest people I knew. There was always enough food on our table to share with other family members who visited. My mom's favorite phrase was, "Where there is a will, there is always a way."

My parents, Louisa and Stanley Flores.

Hurricane Hattie

Hurricane Hattie hit Belize on October 31, 1961. At that time, Dad was the principal of the local school and postmaster. Before the hurricane, my mother prepared some food and baked enough bread for two days. My father packed the essential books and papers in his office in the front part of our home.

Our family had just moved to the new concrete Teacher's house. Our last house was an old wooden house on stilts. We would be safer in the concrete building and had enough food and water for two days. We also said our rosary. We were scared, but all was well because we were prepared for the hurricane. Or so we thought.

That night the hurricane hit, we could hear strong winds blowing. We could only watch as the Caribbean Sea and the Mullins River flooded the land. Our neighbors and other people near us ran into our house for shelter.

The river had been a source of fresh drinking water when there was no rain to fill the water vats. Now that same water was pouring into our house. First, the water covered our ankles, then our knees, and finally, our waists.

Eventually, the men broke open the ceiling. We had to climb up without a ladder or stairs. One of the fathers climbed up first to find a safe spot to sit. Another dad lifted the children while the people in the attic pulled them up. Next, the mothers and older women were pulled up, followed by the men. When the water would have been up to our men's shoulders, we were all safe in the ceiling. Some people were crying, others were praying, and some were clinging to their loved ones. We were all afraid as it continued to rain outside.

My sister Julia rested her feet on the top of the door below us while we waited for the hurricane to pass. Suddenly, the water closed the door with force so fast she did not have time to remove her feet. Three of her toes were caught in the door frame. When the water pushed the door open again, her toes were bleeding. We did not have a first aid kit, so we had to wait for help. By the following day, her injured toes were black and blue. The water continued to rise through the night.

By the following afternoon, the water stopped about one inch below the ceiling. We all thanked God as we watched it going down. We weren't able to see the floor of the house until later that night. When we woke up the next morning, everything in the house was gone. There was no furniture, clothes, or food. We ate the last of our food before we went to sleep the night before.

My dad and some men climbed down to help the women and children from the ceiling. Everyone was hungry, but all were happy to be alive. A few of us went to gather coconuts to eat for breakfast. We drank the coconut water and ate the coconut meat. We all learned how to open fresh or dry coconuts as children.

Some people were injured, but many people in the area hit by Hattie died because they had not found shelter in time. We had no idea how high the water was going to rise. Two days after the weather had taken its toll on the country, helicopters came to drop off food and take the injured. The Red Cross took Julia to the hospital in Dangriga, the area's main town. They amputated her pinky and the two other toes that were injured. In the days that followed, we received more food and clothing. One of the items the Red Cross gave me was a blue blanket. Almost two years after the hurricane, I could not sleep without covering myself from head to toe with that blanket.

A few weeks later, when we gathered firewood to cook, we noticed skeletons clinging to the branches hanging high in a tree. When we returned a few days later, the dads had cut down the branches and buried or burned the dead. It was not easy to identify the people. We knew someone was among the deceased if they had not returned home within a month.

While digging in the yard, my mother found her sewing machine and a few pots and pans. The sewing machine had become rusty, which made it useless. However, the most important thing to her was that our family was safe. I realized that God does love us all and takes care of us in the weeks following Hurricane Hattie.

My two older siblings and I worked with our parents to clean up after the hurricane. Things were not easy, but we knew our parents were doing their best. We were happy to cooperate with them and each other.

My oldest sister, Julia, stayed in Dangriga while the staff at the hospital treated her injuries. By the grace of God, two of my other sisters happened to be going to high school there and were able to help her. My second oldest second sister Sister Joan was in New Orleans, Louisiana. She had left Belize to enter the convent as soon as she graduated from high school. Sister Joan recently celebrated sixty years in the convent.

Louisa and Stanley Flores were hard-working and God-fearing people. My father taught all the children in the Village School, and my Mom taught sewing twice a week. When school reopened after the hurricane, my mother started to cook porridge or pudding for breakfast for all the schoolchildren and prepared powdered milk for them to drink.

My dad was always working or doing community service. He led the prayer on Sundays and took care of the church services when the priest could not be there. Mullins River, where my family lived, was a small village. There was only one priest for the town and surrounding villages. The priest, who also managed the schools in the district, only visited a few times a year.

Even after my dad retired, he was active in Seine Bight, our village. He was the village council chairman for a few years and became the justice of the peace. My dad continued to help in the church and became a minister of the Word with a few other men and women. I also was trained as a minister of the Word to help in the church.

My parents encouraged me to love God, myself, and others. They always believed in helping others, and we saw this every day. My parents taught me that there is no reason why we cannot help others. When we help other human beings, we are also helping ourselves. We all need people; we are social beings.

My Parents Taught Me to Pray

Many people in my village died after Hurricane Hattie. Surviving it taught me to lean on God with prayers. I do not know how I would have faced all my troubles if I did not know God's goodness and love for his people.

My dad worked as a teacher; my mom stayed home with my siblings and me. Even though there was only one salary, there was always cooked food and baked bread on our table. My parents were able to pay for us all to go to high school.

Mom and Dad encouraged us to work hard, but most importantly, we were taught to put God first. I thank God every day that my parents taught us to place our burdens in the hands of the Lord or at the foot of his cross. The older I get, the more I realize that we humans need God daily to see us through life's journey.

Young people today have so much more to deal with than when we were their age. We must teach our children and grandchildren to pray and trust in God's goodness and mercy.

My dad and I were with my mom when she received the Mother of the Year award from St. Alphonsus Church.

In 1994, I received the Mother of the Year award from my church, Our Lady of Montserrat – St. Ambrose, with my daughters, Díonísía and Dían (L-R), at my side.

My cousin Ann Marie and I on our pilgrimage to Israel with my church in 2016.

Frances Flores-Sentino

Part II
The Cookbook

Meal Planning

After my daughter Dían was diagnosed with breast cancer in 2015, she could not tolerate nuts and grains. When I stayed with Dían after her surgery, her dietary restrictions inspired me to prepare some of my mother's naturally grain-free recipes. I have included some of the recipes we both enjoyed.

A few years later, I was diagnosed with prediabetes. I needed to add more beans, vegetables, and fresh fruit to my diet. It was helpful to have oatmeal four mornings a week or in the evening if I was still hungry after supper.

I also began to exercise more and work on reducing my stress. I went on a walk daily and spent more time praying. Sometimes I said the rosary twice a day to manage my stress. Singing some of my favorite church hymns also helped me to feel calm.

In the months following my prediabetes diagnosis, I was reminded that we had small, healthy meals when I was growing up. I am now cooking many of the dishes that my mom made. I did have to make some changes, such as reducing the amount of flour used, adding vegetables, and substituting some ingredients with green bananas.

I recommend planning and preparing your meals for the month or week ahead. Take the time to prepare your meal plan as a teacher would prepare a lesson plan keeping their student's age and needs in mind. When you are done creating your meal plan, hang it up where you can see it.

Some of my other meal-planning suggestions are:
- Reduce fat, sugar, and carbohydrates when possible
- Eat more vegetables and fresh fruits and
- Grow what you can. Some people grow fruits and vegetables on their windowsills in big cities.

Please research and consult your doctor before making any dietary changes. It is your responsibility to take care of yourself. If you do not do it, who will? We should prioritize our health, especially since people are living longer.

Speaking of fruits and vegetables, make sure you always wash them well. If you do not have a store-bought vegetable cleaner, add two cups of water and one cup of vinegar, fresh lime, or lemon juice to a spray bottle. Spray the fruit thoroughly and run under cold water to rinse. I wash my fruit and vegetables even if the container says they are triple-washed or washed five times!

Me and my pepper plant!

Sample Weekly Meal Plan

Sunday

8 AM	Oatmeal with sliced banana on top. Cup of hot cocoa with milk. One slice of whole wheat toast with a small avocado.
12 PM	Steamed chicken with pumpkin, tomatoes, and Brussels sprouts. ½ cup of brown rice. Cup of water with a lemon slice.
4 PM	Chicken, watercress salad with apple, cucumbers, and carrots. Whole wheat pasta.
7 PM	Three bean soup with mixed vegetables and baked salmon. One cup of hot milk.

Monday

8 AM	Oatmeal with dried cranberries; slice of toast with peanut butter; cup of hot cocoa with milk.
10 AM	Three bean soup, dried nuts, and fruits.
12:30 PM	Brown rice, chicken, and mixed vegetables; Water with a slice of lime.
4 PM	A bowl of fruit salad.
7 PM	Rice and beans, baked salmon, spinach and arugula.

Tuesday

8 AM	An egg sandwich on a whole wheat roll with fresh oregano, onions, and tomatoes; green tea.
10 AM	Homemade carrot muffin with split pea and kale soup.
12:30 PM	Chicken soup with mixed vegetables; wild rice and watercress salad.
4 PM	Papaya, orange, apple, and banana smoothie.
7 PM	Chicken cooked with brussels sprouts, red potatoes, onions, and garlic.

Wednesday

8 AM	Oatmeal with nuts and dried fruits. Homemade black bean bread; lemongrass tea.
12 PM	Baked chicken breast, steamed vegetables, and brown rice. 4 oz. of water with 4 oz. of apple juice.
4 PM	Whole wheat pasta salad with beets and mixed vegetables. Steamed fish sautéed with recado, onions, garlic, and parsley flakes.
7 PM	Cabbage salad with carrots, ginger, spinach, and onions. Baked chicken with corn bread or corn tortillas.

Thursday

8 AM	Steamed Louisiana yam or sweet potatoes. Fish in garlic, with black pepper, as well as green and red pepper sauce. Cup of hot cocoa with milk.
12:30 PM	Brown rice with meatballs in tomato sauce and kale.
4 PM	Plain yogurt with flax seeds.
7 PM	Cereal with dried cranberries and nuts. Cup of hot milk.

Friday

8 AM	Oatmeal; slice of whole wheat bread with almond butter; cup of hot cocoa with milk.
10 AM	Three bean soup with mixed vegetables.
12:30 PM	Baked fish, rice and beans, steamed mushrooms with mixed vegetables in garlic sauce
4 PM	Fruit salad and water with a slice of lemon
7 PM	Baked salmon and brown rice; watercress salad with cucumbers, spinach, and carrots

Saturday

Leftovers All Day

Mom's Recipes

There are two of my mom's recipes that I have been trying to recreate: cassava pudding and powder bun. My dad used to say that my mom made the best powder bun, and he was right! To my delight, I finally mastered my mom's cassava pudding on Thanksgiving in 2018. It was perfect! My family and friends were happy to taste the real thing. I am still working on perfecting the powder bun recipe to make for Christmas.

My siblings and I have our mother's recipes to keep us connected. We also share what we remember with each other. When I moved to the United States, my sisters would tell me how much our dad missed the desserts I used to make!

Now that my parents are no longer with us, I go to the kitchen and cook or bake when I think about them. Knowing that the joy and peace I remember are still with me makes me smile.

Basic Sorrel Drink

Growing up in Belize, my mom made sorrel for Easter, Christmas, Garifuna Settlement Day, and other special occasions. She harvested the fruit from the plants in her garden. We also used it as a filling for tarts and jam.

I have continued the tradition of making sorrel for special occasions with my family.

7.5-8 oz. natural dried sorrel fruit

¼ cup fresh grated ginger or 1 tsp ginger powder

2 or 3 star anise

1 three-inch cinnamon stick or

1 TB of ground cinnamon

1 cup brown sugar (optional)

Put all the ingredients in a large pot and add one and a half gallons of water. Bring the water to a boil and cook for five to ten minutes. Remove from heat. Sweeten after the drink cools. Drink hot or cold.

Split Pea Soup

2 medium onions

2 cups split peas

4 cups water

1 tsp fresh basil or powder

1 tsp garlic powder

1 13.5 oz can of coconut milk

2 medium sweet potatoes or Louisiana yams

¼ tsp salt

¼ tsp black pepper

1 head of garlic with eight or more cloves

Soak dry split peas in 3 cups of water (or until covered) in advance for less cooking time. First, put peas, water, and garlic in the pot. Next, peel the sweet potatoes and cut them into even sizes. Add them to the cooked split peas with basil and salt. Finally, slowly pour one cup of coconut milk into the pot while stirring. Cook in an open skillet over medium heat for 45 minutes.

Meatballs in Black Sauce (Reano Negro)

1 lb ground beef

½ sweet pepper, diced

¼ tsp black pepper

¼ tsp oregano

1 medium onion, chopped

3 cloves of garlic

½ cup oatmeal or breadcrumbs

4 hard-boiled eggs or one for each person

½ a whole chicken, cut into pieces

¼ of black recado package

1 Tbsp of oil

2 cups of water

Mix ground beef, sweet pepper, black pepper, oats (or breadcrumbs), and oregano in a bowl—mold the mixture into meatballs. Season the chicken with your preferred seasonings. Grease a baking sheet for the meatballs and pan for the chicken with a tablespoon of oil. Bake both at 350° for 30 minutes.

Boil eggs until they are hard-boiled. Drain the hot water from the pot and add cold water. When cool, peel off the shells and put the eggs to the side.

Mix the black recado and water in a pot. Add the meatball and chicken with the onions and garlic to the pot after baking. Cook for 25 minutes. When it is time to serve the meal, add an egg to each plate with the meatballs, chicken, and gravy. Serve with tortillas (corn or flour) or rice of your choice.

Green Banana and Cornmeal Porridge

1 cup cornmeal

1 green banana

¼ cup – 1/cup milk (optional)

3 cups water

¼ tsp ground cinnamon

½ tsp ground nutmeg

Stir cornmeal in three cups of water in a pot over low heat; bring to a boil. Add grated green banana to the pot a little at a time. Next, add cinnamon and nutmeg. Stir for a few minutes, then cover for ten minutes to cook well. Add the preferred amount of milk to individual bowls. Makes four servings.

Coconut Crust

For dough:

1 egg

1 egg white mixed with 1 Tbsp of water

2 cups flour

½ cup water (add more if needed)

1 tsp baking powder

½ tsp baking soda

For coconut filling:

1 medium coconut, grated or 1 cup of shredded coconut

½ tsp cinnamon

½ tsp nutmeg

1 tsp vanilla

¾ cup of brown sugar

1 cup of water

Mix the ingredients for the dough in a bowl. Mold the dough into eight small balls and let rest for 30 minutes. While the dough is resting, add the coconut-filling ingredients to a medium cast-iron pot or skillet. Cook on high heat to bring to a boil, then lower to medium heat for about 15 minutes. Stir occasionally. Remove the pot from the stove and let it cool to room temperature.

Once the coconut filling is cooled, flatten the dough balls until they look like tortillas. Place one tablespoon of the filling in each dough round. Fold the circle in half and use a fork to flatten the open side of each coconut crust. Brush egg white mixture on top of each pastry. Place on a baking sheet and bake in the oven at 350° for 30 minutes or until brown. Let cool to room temperature before serving.

Banana Bread

6 ripe bananas, medium

1 ½ cups flour

¼ tsp nutmeg

¼ tsp cinnamon

½ can of coconut milk

1 cup of water

1/3 cup margarine or ¼ cup of olive or coconut oil

1 cup mixed fruit pre-soaked in 1 cup cranberry juice

(or ¼ cup raisins soaked in ½ cup warm water)

1 tsp baking powder

1 tsp baking soda

Preheat the oven to 400° for ten minutes. Grease the loaf pan with a teaspoon of coconut oil or margarine. Blend all the ingredients in a big bowl and pour the mixture into the pan. Bake at 350° for 25 minutes or until golden brown.

Green Banana Pancake

2 large or 3 small green bananas

1 tsp baking powder

½ tsp baking soda

1 cup flour

¼ tsp pepper

½ cup coconut milk

½ cup water

½ tsp minced garlic, fresh or dry

Grate the green bananas in a large bowl. Mix in the other ingredients. Preheat a 10-inch cast iron pan and add a small amount of oil. Use a pot spoon to pour one serving into the pan. Cook until the edges are brown, then flip over with a spatula. Cook for another four minutes or until brown. Makes six to seven pancakes.

Pumpkin Bread

1 16oz can of pumpkin

8 oz milk of choice

½ cup dried cranberries (soak in warm water for 15 min)

1 tsp powder

1 tsp baking soda

1 tsp of coconut oil

3 cups flour

1 egg

¾ cups nuts or pumpkin seeds

Preheat the oven to 400° for ten minutes. Mix all ingredients in a large bowl. Grease the loaf pan with the coconut oil before pouring in the mixture. Bake at 350° for 25 minutes.

Green Banana & Pink Salmon Cake

3 green bananas

1 16oz can of salmon

1 medium – onion, grated

½ tsp ginger, freshly grated or powdered

½ tsp cilantro or oregano

¼ tsp cayenne pepper

¼ cup of preferred oil (other than olive oil)

Homemade pesto (recipe on page 56)

Grate the green bananas into a large bowl. Mix in the other ingredients. Preheat a 10-inch cast iron pan at medium heat. Add one tablespoon of oil to the pan. Add another tablespoon if the pan becomes dry. Use a pot spoon to pour one serving of the batter into the pan. Cook until the edge of the pancake is brown, and then flip over with a spatula. Cook for another four minutes or until brown. Makes six to seven salmon cakes.

Pesto

2 cloves fresh garlic

½ cup fresh basil or parsley

½ cup walnut

Purée all ingredients together until ingredients are thoroughly blended.

Black Fruit Cake

1 cup butter or olive oil

2 cups brown sugar

5 eggs

3 ½ cups flour

3 tsp baking powder

15 oz of applesauce

½ pint caramel coloring or burnt sugar

1 tsp nutmeg, clove, or allspice powder

2 lbs mixed fruit

2 cups brandy or rum

½ lb raisins

½ tsp cinnamon

2 oz cherries

Soak fruit in 1 cup of warm water and 1 cup of brandy or rum overnight.

Mix the butter and sugar until it becomes creamy. Add one egg at a time to the mixture and beat until fluffy. Stir all dry ingredients (flour, baking powder, and spices) in a different container and add the cream mixture.

Stir in fruits, nuts, and raisins soaked in brandy or rum. Add caramel coloring or burnt sugar. Bake at 350° for 60 minutes or until golden brown. Let the cake cool for 10 mins, then remove it from the baking pan and place it in a container with a cover. Leave to cool for another 20 minutes, then pour 1 cup of brandy or rum over the cake and let it soak overnight.

My Mom's Stewed Green Papaya

1 medium green papaya or 5 small green papayas

1 ½ cups brown sugar

1 tsp cloves

1 tsp cinnamon powder

¼ cup freshly grated ginger

1 tsp vanilla

2 tsp grated Nutmeg

3 cups water

Cook papayas, sugar, and grated ginger in three cups of water for 15 minutes. Add all other spices and vanilla. When the papaya is soft, lower the heat and let it simmer. After 45 minutes, raise to medium heat stirring every five minutes. When the sauce has the consistency of syrup, turn off the stove.

Eat with fresh cornbread, whole wheat bread, or flatbread during the Easter season. You can also cook papaya as a vegetable to be served with meat. It's best to prepare it ahead of time, bottle it and store it in the refrigerator.

Cassava Pudding

4 lbs cassava, grated

1 1/2 cups sugar

2 cans of coconut milk (fill the empty cans with water and add to the mixture)

½ tsp lime zest

2 Tbsps baking powder

1 Tbsp vanilla

1 Tbsp cinnamon (ground)

1 Tbsp nutmeg (ground)

Mix the ingredients and pour into a pan lightly greased with cooking oil. Bake at 350° in the lower part of the oven for 30 mins to get a brown crust. Then bake for 30 minutes on the upper shelf to brown the top.

Cabbage Salad

1 head of cabbage, thinly sliced

1 onion, diced

1 Tbsp black pepper

½ cup parsley

1 Tbsp garlic powder

1 Tbsp ginger, grated

2 medium carrots, peeled and diced

2 cups water

½ cup of sliced almonds or other nuts (optional)

Sauté onion and cabbage. Add 1 cup water and all other ingredients except the almonds. Cover the pot and allow it to steam at a low flame. In ten minutes, stir and add the other cup of water. Add pepper and salt to taste. Serve hot. If including nuts, toast and add before serving.

Festive Rice

1 ½ cups Rice

2 Tbsps yellow ginger or turmeric

1 tsp regular ginger

2 medium carrots, grated

8 oz fresh or frozen green peas

1 onion, finely chopped

1 ½ cup coconut milk

2 cups of water

Place all ingredients (except the water) in a large pot or rice cooker. Add water until it is at least two inches above the ingredients. Stir well and leave to cook for 30 minutes. Serve hot.

Spinach Rice

1 ½ cups brown rice

3 cups water

1 cup finely chopped fresh or frozen spinach

1 small onion, chopped

1 Tbsp garlic powder

Cook rice with water, onion, and garlic powder in an open rice cooker or a pot without a cover for 15 minutes. Add spinach and stir well to evenly distribute the spinach. Let cook for 15 more minutes.

My Version of Scones or Irish Soda Bread

3 cups flour

1/2 tsp ground cinnamon

½ tsp ground ginger

½ tsp ground nutmeg

1 small box of raisins (1.33 oz.) presoaked in warm water for 10 minutes

1 tsp baking powder

1 tsp baking soda

2 Tbsp 100% unsweetened cocoa

1 15 or 16-oz can of unsweetened applesauce

1 Tbsp coconut oil

1 cup of 2% fat milk or ½ can of evaporated milk

1 egg

½ cup wheat germ

Mix ingredients in a large bowl until fluffy. Grease a cupcake pan or cookie sheet and scoop the batter onto it. Make sure there is enough space between each scone. Bake for 45-60 minutes at 350°.

Fruit as a Side Dish or Dessert

1. Slice several kinds of fresh fruit (or use canned fruit without syrup) and put them into an attractive bowl.
2. Add a small amount of sherbet, sorbet, or low-fat yogurt as a topping.

My Bean Dishes

Beans have always been a staple in my diet. My mom often used beans as a meat substitute. Here are some ways that I prepare beans:

1. Salad - Beans, cucumber, carrots, spinach, or sautéed cabbage. Use one or more types of beans. It doesn't need any dressing and is filling.
2. Pancakes - Add whole wheat flour, eggs, and very little oil. Mix with beans of choice.
3. Brownies or bread.
4. Rice and beans.
5. Stew beans with green banana dumplings.
6. Fried beans - using as little oil as possible.

Part III
My Nutrition Workshop Notes

The following notes are from workshops at the senior centers I attend.

How to Build a Better Meal to Avoid Diabetes

1. Pasta: top spaghetti with meatless tomato sauce and steamed vegetables. Make lasagna with low-fat cheese and a layer of spinach or broccoli.
2. Rice or other grains: Serve brown rice with stir-fried vegetables. Add rice to vegetable soup or chili.
3. Try whole grains like barley, couscous, wild rice, millet, kasha bulgur, or quinoa.
4. Make whole wheat pita bread pizzas topped with veggies.
5. Top baked potatoes with steamed vegetables and nonfat sour cream.
6. Make a delicious stew with plenty of potatoes, carrots, and onions.
7. Eat sweet potatoes instead of white potatoes.

Foods To Avoid Before Bedtime

Grapefruit - it is too acidic and can interact with some medications.
Celery - has a high-water content and may cause waking up during the night. Eat at least 90 minutes before going to bed.
Tomatoes – are rich in tyramine and boost brain activity, which delays sleep. Other foods with tyramine are eggplant, red wine, soy sauce, and aged cheeses such as brie.

Eat At Least Two Hours Before Bedtime

Foods high in fat and fried foods take longer to digest and may interfere with sleep.

Eat Three hours before bedtime

Bean chili - Eat chili earlier in the day. The body has difficulty digesting beans, preventing a good night's sleep. It may cause gas pains. Also, avoid gassy vegetables, such as Brussels sprouts, broccoli, cabbage, asparagus, and cauliflower, before bedtime due to their indigestible sugar.

Eat 2-4 Hours Before Bedtime

Too much sugar will cause blood sugar to rise and spike, then fall rapidly as the body releases insulin to control the sugar. These fluctuations make it difficult to stay asleep.

Have It for Lunch

Dark chocolate - helps keep the heart healthy. Have it 4-6 hours before bedtime. Don't nibble before going to bed if you are sensitive to caffeine.

Alcohol - You may doze off at first, but it disrupts sleep later in the night and robs you of rapid eye movement. Lack of REM sleep impairs concentration and memory.

Foods That Lead to a Good Night's Sleep

1. Tart cherries - its juice contains antioxidants and melatonin.

2. Turkey - contains the amino acid tryptophan, which produces relaxation and sound sleep. Chicken, tuna, shrimp, and salmon also contain tryptophan.

3. Chamomile tea - it is caffeine free and helps with relaxation.

4. ½ a Banana - has vitamin B6. It helps the body produce serotonin which helps with sound sleep.

5. Almonds - are high in magnesium, which relaxes the body.

6. Epsom salt - relaxes you at night when added to your bath.

Serving Sizes for One

A single serving of:	Is about the size of:
An Apple	A tennis ball
Chips or pretzels	A handful
Grilled Fish	A checkbook
Chicken, Beef, Pork, or Tukey	A deck of cards
Pasta	One ice cream scoop
Steamed Rice	One cup
Vegetables (cooked)	The palm of your hand
Vegetables (raw)	Your fist

About the Author

Frances Flores-Sentino is a proud Garifuna woman from Seine Bight Village in Belize, Central America. She is the youngest of Stanley and Louisa Flores' seven children. Her mom was a homemaker and a talented gardener. Her dad was a teacher and a very active member of the community.

Frances taught in Belize for several years. She was introduced to the Montessori teaching method while discerning with the Sisters of Charity of Nazareth in Kentucky. In 1981, Frances moved to New York and became a registered medical assistant. Frances later became a certified Montessori teacher. She taught at the Nazareth Nursery preschool for 30 years. She was a head teacher when she retired in 2015.

Frances is a member of the Tompkins Park Writer's Association, the All Saints Roman Catholic Church, and a retired registered medical assistant with the American Medical Technologists (AMT). She is also a lifetime associate of the Sisters of Charity of Nazareth. Frances has two adult daughters and a granddaughter.

Frances being observed teaching a 1st-grade class in Belize while studying for her First-Class Teacher exam.

Frances at the National Catholic Educational Association conference

www.ingramcontent.com/pod-product-compliance
Lightning Source LLC
Chambersburg PA
CBHW060420050426
42449CB00009B/2057